Spirited Child and
Stay Safe Inc Presents:
# Sit and Sing

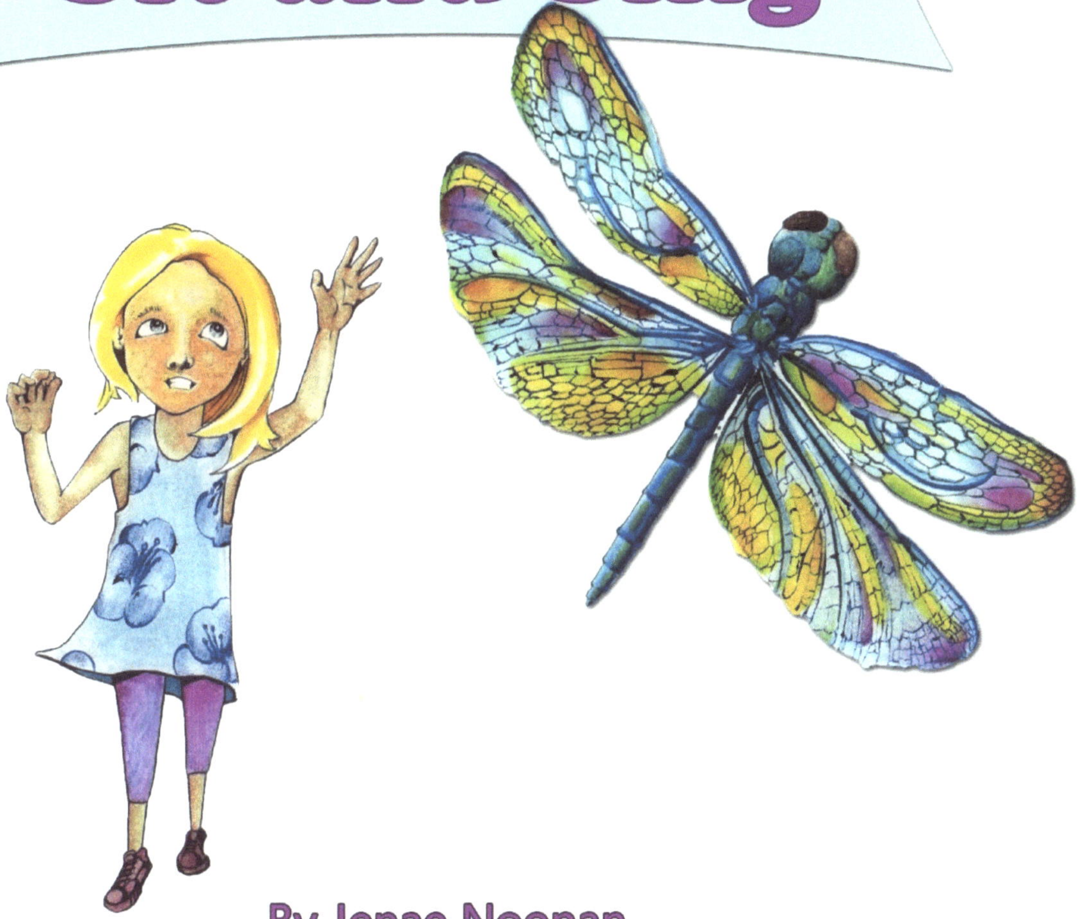

By Jenae Noonan
Illustrated by Johnnie Dominguez

Illustrations by Johnnie Dominguez

Art design by Jenae Noonan and Johnnie Dominguez

© Stay Safe Inc and Victory Publishing

ISBN-13: 978-0692992739 (Victory)

ISBN-10: 0692992731

Victory Publishing, Unites States

All rights reserved 2017

Sit and Sing ™

One morning Rossi said, "Lets go on a hike."

The mom replied, "That is a great idea," and she packed a backpack full of water while dad helped the children pick appropriate shoes. They packed the car and headed to the lake.

On the car ride mom and dad were talking to the children about what they might see.

"Rossi, what do you think we will find?" the mom asked.

"We will see ducks and brids," Rossi answered excitedly.

"Hollin, what do you think you will see? The dad asked.

"I will see the same ducks as Rossi and a dragonfly. I love dragonflies, they fly really fast all around; and dogs, we will see dogs. Hopefully we don't see a dog catching a dragonfly. I don't think dogs can catch them. Dad can dogs catch dragonflies?" Hollin did not wait for the answer. She just kept talking about all the things she was going to see at the lake the whole drive there.

When the family got to the lake they reminded the children to stay close and they began their hike.

Along the way Hollin saw a dragon fly and stopped walking to stare at it. The rest of the family kept walking.

After a few minutes Rossi looked back and saw that Hollin had fallen behind and she ran back to get her. When she got there Hollin showed her the dragonfly. Rossi, unamused, told Hollin to hurry up but when she looked up she could no longer see their mom and dad. Rossi realised they were lost.

Hollin said, "Don't worry Rossi we will go find them," and she began to walk off.

Rossi grabbed her hand and told her they needed to stay put. She reminded her that if you ever get lost you sit where you are and you sing. Hollin insisted on going to find mom and dad. She was scared and told Rossi maybe they were playing hide and seek and wanted us to find them. Rossi told her not to be scared and asked what song she thought mom and dad would hear them singing.

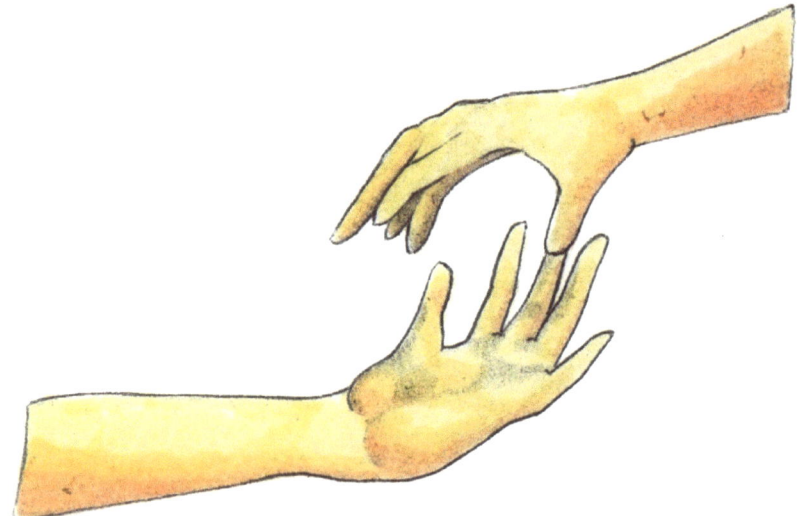

The children sat where they were and started singing.

In no time at all both mom and dad came around the corner and found their children sitting and singing.

Mom and dad were so happy!

"I am so glad you stayed here. It made finding you easier." Mom said as she picked up Hollin and gave her a hug.

"I am so glad you sat down and were singing. We could hear you and we knew where to find you." Dad cheerfully explained.

The family walked back to the car and went for ice cream to celebrate their children's decision to sit and sing.

# Letter to the Parents

Dear Parents'

    The most important thing to us is our children's safety. Teaching young children the safest way to handle situations will help keep children safer. It is important to teach a child to stay in one place if they are lost. Children learn through play. When a parent plays hide and seek with their children it teaches them to "go find" their parents when they cannot see them. If your child were to get lost in a crowded place the learned behavior of looking for you can become dangerous. Teaching your child to stay in one place will make it easier for the parent to find them. Most parents, after realizing their child is lost, will retrace their steps or return to the place they last saw their child. Teaching your child to stay there can help the search tremendously. Also it is important to teach your child to stay there no matter what. If an adult asks them if they can help, teach your child to have the adult stay with them there. ALWAYS stay put!

    Singing also helps calm the nerves of the child and helps you find them as well. If you were at a mall and heard your child singing their favorite song you would be able to locate them quicker. My mom was in an airport once. She saw a little boy crying and asked if he was lost. He confirmed that he was and she asked what his favorite song was. The two of them sat and began to sing Twinkle Twinkle. The boy had stopped crying and was enjoying singing. A few other parents saw what was happening and had their children sit with my mom and the boy. By the time the mother returned to find the boy it looked like a story time of 5 children and my mom. The boy was returned to the mom safely and happy!

www.ingramcontent.com/pod-product-compliance
Lightning Source LLC
Chambersburg PA
CBHW041542040426
42446CB00002B/201